Document Exercise Workbook
for
WESTERN CIVILIZATION
Fourth Edition
VOLUME I: To 1715

Donna L. Van Raaphorst
Cuyahoga Community College

 **Wadsworth**
Thomson Learning.

Australia • Canada • Denmark • Japan • Mexico • New Zealand • Philippines
Puerto Rico • Singapore • South Africa • Spain • United Kingdom • United States

For more information, contact
Wadsworth/Thomson Learning
10 Davis Drive
Belmont, CA 94002-3098
USA
www.wadsworth.com

International Headquarters
Thomson Learning
290 Harbor Drive, 2nd Floor
Stamford, CT 06902-7477
USA

UK/Europe/Middle East
Thomson Learning
Berkshire House
168-173 High Holborn
London WC1V 7AA
United Kingdom

Asia
Thomson Learning
60 Albert Complex
Singapore 189969

Canada
Nelson/Thomson Learning
1120 Birchmount Road
Scarborough, Ontario M1K 5G4
Canada

ISBN 0-534-56846-7

For Paul, whose help along the way
would have made it eminently better.

Contents

Vol. I

Foreword

To The Student

To The Instructor

Foreword

The genesis of this work has been twenty some years of classroom instruction. Throughout this time period my students have been my best teachers and in no case is this more so than with the revisions in this edition.

Many individuals helped to make these volumes possible. Of particular note are Clark Baxter, Sharon Adams-Poore, and Cherie Hackelberg of Wadsworth Publishing.

Equally supportive were a couple individuals on the Western Campus of Cuyahoga Community College. Of special note are Ms. Mikki Shackelton, a former student and Mr. John Twist, book center manager. Special appreciation need also be given to the word processor for this edition, Ms. Larraine Stranca. Last but not least I am particularly grateful to my trusted and true friend Mary Kay Howard of John Carroll University for our numerous "brainstorming sessions." Without their assistance, aid, and cooperation this work would not have been possible.

To The Student

This supplement was written with you in mind. Specifically, it was designed to complement the textbook you are reading in your Western Civilization course.

The method of organization herein is chronological and the exercises that accompany the documents will progress from the relatively simple to the far more complex. The documents reflect the wide range of materials historians use in attempting to reconstruct the past. If you begin using this supplement when your coursework commences and continue to use it throughout the duration of your survey study of Western Civilization, you will develop a better understanding of historical source materials and of how historians study history.

The actual doing of history, the essence of this supplement, will hopefully excite some of you enough that you might wish to do and learn even more. To that end this edition has included a new section called:

- ***CHALLENGE YOURSELF FURTHER***

Technology can also enrich your study of history and with that in mind, several of the exercises in this edition include sections entitled:

- ***YOUR INTERNET CONNECTION***

Log on and enjoy.

To The Instructor

The materials within are arranged in a typical chronological fashion, but this book attempts to be more than simply another collection of documents. It endeavors to engage the student in a study of the past through a series of carefully constructed exercises using primary sources. These exercises are intended to develop thinking skills appropriate to the study of history. As such, they progress from those relatively simple in nature to those far more complex. More importantly, the exercises are ultimately aimed, as Russel H. Hvolbek has aptly written, for "the primary purpose of teaching history and the humanities (which) is to make students more aware of how their lives connect to the past human experience." This objective cannot be achieved by simply acquiring a body of knowledge. Students will come much closer to this goal if they learn how to seek out information and if they learn how to use this information. Hvolbek informs us that this is our ultimate responsibility in reevaluating how we teach our discipline with the provocative title of his essay--"History and Humanities: Teaching as Destructive of Certainty." (AHA Perspectives, January, 1991)

In this edition I have changed some of the documents and endeavored to add further clarification to some of the questions. On occasion I have supplemented questions with particularly challenging assignments for especially inquisitive and interested students. This question will appear under the heading:

- ***CHALLENGE YOURSELF FURTHER***

I have also added an Internet component to enhance understand. This appears throughout this book under the heading:

- ***YOUR INTERNET CONNECTION***

Chapter I
The Nature of History

Before you read this important introductory chapter, write your definition of history on a piece of paper and then put your response aside. When you have finished reading this chapter, examine anew your original thoughts. Compare the differences you find. Think about these differences.

This simple exercise is intended to challenge your presumptions about history. History is not what many of you think it to be. It is not the acquisition of a body of information--names, dates, places, events--simply to be memorized and then shortly forgotten. History is much more. History is far more difficult, far more thought-provoking, far more profound, far more exciting, and more important, far more meaningful to your lives. In fact, one could argue that it is the most important subject you will ever study. When examined and understood properly, history provides us with insights into the fundamental questions that have always concerned humanity beginning with who am I and why am I here? When you understand history you will have become an informed, literate, insightful, thinking human being.

Understood in this way, history would be classified as part of a larger group of disciplines identified as the humanities. An even more thoughtful way to think of history, along with the other humanities, is as the <u>Report of the Colloquium on the Humanities and the American People</u>, has done:

We identify them, rather, with certain ways of thinking--of inquiring, evaluating, judging, finding, and articulating meaning . . . . They are taken together, the necessary resources of a reflective approach to life. The value of a reflective approach can be best appreciated by considering the alternative: a life unilluminated by imagination, uninformed by history, unguided by reasoning--in short, the "unexamined life" that Socrates described as not worth living . . . .(1)

In order that these statements reflect more than grandiloquent expressions of a historian about their chosen discipline, three important questions must be addressed. They are the following: What is history?; How does the historian proceed?; and, What is history for?

A logical place to turn in your attempt to answer the first question, "What is history?," would be a dictionary of word origins or a book of word histories. In so doing you are examining the etymology of the word--its history or its origins. Etymologically, then, history simply denotes "knowledge." This should be interesting for you to discover because the most simplistic understanding of history is often that it is the accumulation of information. To arrive at the more complex aspects of our word, a more specific modern meaning must be uncovered.

The modern story (frequently another common definition of history) begins with the Greek word histor, meaning "learned man." In turn, histor is a descendant of the Indo-European word wid, which is defined as to "know" or "see." This led to the English word wit and the Latin word videre, meaning "see." From histor the word historia evolved and, for you, its meaning is of utmost significance. The definition of historia is "knowledge obtained by inquiring, or a written account of one's inquiries."(2) History, then is a process of inquiring. Specifically the historian, as well as the student of history, inquires into the past and records his or her findings.

Use of the word inquire says something important because it implies a process of asking questions that leads to an interpretation of the evidence. A process is doing and that is the essence of what this small book is trying to teach you--how to do history rather than be a passive recipient of information.(3) In order to do history, you must learn how to ask good questions. Obviously the historian (in this case you) proceeds by asking questions about things that happened in the past. Simple enough, right? Not really, not after you have thought about it momentarily.

Whether you realize it or not, some questions are not appropriate to the discipline of history. For example, you would not ask questions about the past failure of your compact disk player to work properly. Questions not germane to humans, their activities, their institutions, their culture, their economy are inappropriate for historical investigation. However, the main difficulty confronting historians isn't eliminating unimportant or unanswerable questions. It is, instead, choosing from among the important ones.

Generally speaking, the important questions historians ask of their evidence, called sources, are--the who; the why; the when; the where; and, most important of all, the so what? Reflect for a moment on this as you read the following ideas of the well-known Yale historian, Professor Robin W. Winks, on history and asking good questions:

> History is, fundamentally, applied common sense. History begins in the fascination of discreet fact. History is curiosity, a desire to poke and pry to get answers to questions. History is asking good questions. [But not all these questions will, or should, be answered--save one.] The most challenging question, a damaging question that should be asked of any lecturer who ever spelled out a theory, is to look them straight in the eye and say, "Yes, but so what?" It's a paralyzing question. It's soul-destroying. And yet the historian must be able to answer the question.(4)

Mention of sources has been made several times. Historical sources are found in a variety of forms and places. In fact, historical sources, evidence of the past, are everywhere around you. Here are some examples--letters, maps, photographs, cemeteries, reports, personal diaries, buildings, recordings. The list is all but endless, but most traditionally the historian works with written sources, which are commonly referred to as documents. A document is defined as "a thing existing here and now, of such a kind that the historian, by thinking about it, can get answers to the questions he asks about past events."(5)

Generally speaking, when the historian uses the word document, he or she means "primary source" material. This means a record of the actual words of someone who either participated or witnessed whatever is being described. Primary sources are one of two basic types of evidence the historian uses in reconstructing the past. The other is referred to as a "secondary source." A secondary source is the interpretation of an individual who did not participate or witness whatever is being descibed, but who investigated the primary source(s), e.g., an historian.

If good questions need to be formulated in order to interpret your source materials, you also need to examine your evidence carefully for bias, for accuracy, for content. Suppose you were to write a biography of Winston Churchill. Would it be wise to rely only on funeral orations; family memoirs; the opinions of political opponents? Why not? In other words, as you evaluate your sources, you need to consider the circumstances under which they were written. What might have been the motive of the author? What was the relationship of the writer to the individual in question? What was the relationship of the author to the person, the place, the event, the time in question? One source needs to be checked against another to try and establish as full and as accurate a picture of the past as possible. As possible, of course, implies incomplete. Did you ever realize or consider this fact?

Think of it in terms of the philosophical issue of the forest and the tree. In that forest how many trees exist? How many of those trees can you actually observe? Even if you say one and you are standing under it, how many of its limbs can you observe; how many of its actual branches; and, how many of its leaves? When you consider this, you can perhaps begin to comprehend the true meaning of as possible and incomplete. The author Janet Malcolm expressed it beautifully when she wrote, "in a work of nonfiction we almost never know the truth of what happened. The ideal of unmediated reporting is regularly achieved only in fiction, where the writer faithfully reports on what is going on in his imagination. . . ."(6)

One final aspect concerning the question of how the historian proceeds needs to be addressed. That question concerns itself with the matter of organization--how are the source materials discovered about the past to be organized in such a way that significant information becomes apparent? Examination of this issue has demonstrated certain basic human activities that clearly stand out and answer basic questions. These activities fall into the following categories: political; economic; social; religious; scientific; cultural; and, intellectual. Some might also include technological and artistic. Remember these as you progress through the various exercises in this book and as you study and learn for your history course.

Almost fifty years ago now, R. G. Collingwood, a Professor of Philosophy at Oxford and a practicing historian, asked and answered the final question under consideration in this chapter: "What is history for?" Conceding it to be the most difficult and highly individualistic in nature, Collingwood nonetheless wrote,

> My answer is that history is 'for' human self-knowledge. It is generally thought to be of importance to man that he should know himself: where knowing himself means knowing not his merely personal peculiarities . . . but his nature as man. Knowing yourself means knowing first, what it is to be a man; secondly, knowing what it is to be the kind of man you are; and thirdly, knowing what it is to be the man you are and nobody else is. Knowing yourself means knowing what you can do; and since nobody knows what he can do until he tries, the only clue to what man can do is what man has done. The value of history, then, is that it teaches us what man has done and thus what man is.(7)

Endnotes

1. Merrill D. Peterson, <u>The Humanities and the American Promise</u>, Report of the Colloquium on the Humanities and the American People (Austin, Texas: Texas Committee for the Humanities, 1987), 2-3.

2. <u>Dictionary of Word Origins</u>, s.v. "history," and <u>The Merriam-Webster New Book of Word Histories</u>, s.v. "history."

3. Finlay McQuade, "What is <u>doing</u> a discipline?" (Waltham, MA: The College Board, n.d.).

4. "For Sleuth, History is Where He Finds It," <u>The Plain Dealer</u>, 11 February 1990.

5. R. G. Collingwood, <u>The Idea of History</u> (New York: Oxford University Press, 1946; A Galaxy Book, 1956), 10.

6. Janet Malcolm, "The Silent Woman - III," <u>The New Yorker</u>, 23 & 30 August 1993, 138.

7. Collingwood, <u>The Idea of History</u>, 10.

Chapter II
Applying the Basics to Historical Sources

Now that you have addressed the essentials and come to terms with a new understanding and appreciation of the complexities of history, you should be ready to actually try your hand at doing some history. In this chapter your exercises will deal with two types of source materials. Scholars of very early history frequently have to rely on other than strictly written materials like documents. It is important for you to understand how to use a variety of source materials even in your attempt to understand the modern world. Consider how many letters you have written lately? Do you keep a written diary?

Your first exercise will focus on a coin, what is commonly classified as an artifact. Coins have a history of their own; one that begins in the western part of Asia Minor in an early civilization called Lydia. Establishing a brief hegemony over Asia Minor from the middle of the 7th to the middle of the 6th century B.C., the Lydians are believed to have invented metallic coinage. Prior to this, jewelry was probably the closest thing to money.(1) Lydians are also responsible for establishing the first permanent retail shops and together these two important contributions to civilization played a role as catalyst in bringing about a commercial revolution helping to transform 6th century B.C. Greek civilization.

Let us suppose you find the coin pictured at the bottom of this page in the ruins of a very ancient civilization about which you know absolutely nothing. You are able to decipher the language for it is very similar to your own. However, you don't understand how this came to be. Study the coin carefully and then do the following:

1. List five to ten things you believe you can determine about this civilization.

2. Take your list and categorize it according to those most commonly used by historians to organize their information. Remember what they are?--political; economic; social; religious; scientific; cultural; and, intellectual.

Are you surprised by how much can be determined with one piece of evidence? Did you ever think of coins as an historical source? Actually, they are often invaluable to the historian. For instance, almost no records exist to inform us about the Parthian dynasty in 247 B.C. The Parthians were originally a nomadic people from central Asia, who at some point in history entered Iran (ancient Persia). Apparently they were at their peak of power about the end of the second century B.C. Tucked between two far greater powers--Rome to the west and China to the east--they were able to control at least a part of the great Silk Route and act as middle-men between their mightier neighbors. Inscriptions on coins and potsherds (pieces of broken earthen pots) have helped to corroborate the only other source materials available: the findings of archaeologists and subjective accounts of classical Greek and Roman texts.(2) Are you convinced?

Begin working with a somewhat more conventional piece of historical evidence, one that might be considered a document yet it was discovered by modern archaeologists who were digging in Mesopotania for very ancient civilizations around a century ago. At a place called Nineveh, as well as numerous other old Assyrian cities, these archaeologists discovered a rich find of clay tablets. Amazingly these tablets were inscribed with an unusual wedge-shaped writing called cuneiform.

Originally it was thought that the script was Semitic in origin, but after experts figured out how to decipher it, they concluded that the writing was not in fact originated by the Assyrian Semites. Indeed they surmised that the Assyrians had taken over the cuneiform script from a people called Sumerians. The scholor who is credited with this discovery was a 19th century expert of ancient Mesopotainia named Jules Oppert. Thus after about 2000 years of oblivion Sumer became a major source of continuous excavation for well over three-quarters of a century. Despite the richness of these finds cuneiform was the most important contributions made by the Sumerians to civilization

Some experts maintain it is the earliest known system of writing in human history and it served as the instrument of written communication throughout western Asia for over 2000 year.

From this point on, whenever you are working with a document, always perform the following procedures:

- o   Have a dictionary by your side. You cannot understand a document if you do not understand the vocabulary.

- o   As you read through the document, circle all unfamiliar words and look them up in your dictionary.

- o   As you read through the document, look for the important ideas that relate to the question or questions you are seeking to answer (the who?; the why?; the when?; the where?; and the so what?). Underline them.

- o   Write these ideas out in your own words. In this way you will better understand them.

Remember these procedures as you make your way through the sections of the Tablets provided on the next few pages. Write and work on them as they are designed with that in mind.

DOCUMENT

I.   Creation of Man

[An exchange between Nammu, the goddess of the ocean, and Enki, her son, the water god and god of wisdom.]

> "Oh my son, rise from your bed, from you wise work.
>
> Fashion servants of the gods, may they produce their doubles."

"O my mother, the creature whose name you uttered, it exists,

Bind upon it the image of the gods;

Mix the heart of the clay that is over the abyss,

The good and princely fashioners will thicken the clay,

You, do you bring the limbs into existence;

Ninmah (the earth-mother goddess) will work above you,

The goddesses (of birth). . . .will stand by you at your fashioning;

O my mother, decree its (the newborn's) fate,

Ninmah will bind upon it the image of the gods,

It is Man. . . ."

II.   **The Flood**

Ziusudra, standing at [the holy wall's] side, listened.

"Stand by the wall at my left side. . .,

By the wall I will say a word to you, take my word,

Give ear to my instructions:

By our [word missing on tablet] . . .a flood will sweep over the cult centers;

To destroy the seed of mankind [words missing]

Is the decision, the word of the assembly of the gods?

By the word commanded by An and Enlil,

Its kingship, its rule (will be put to an end)."

All the windstorms, exceedingly powerful, attacked as one,

At the same time, the flood sweeps over the cult centers.

After, for seven days and seven nights, The Flood had swept over the land,

And the huge boat had been tossed about by the windstorms

on the great waters.

Utu came forth, who sheds light on heaven and earth,

Ziusudra opened a window on the huge boat,

The hero Utu brought his rays into the giant boat

Ziusudra, the king, prostrated himself before Utu.

The king kills an oz, slaughters a sheep.

An and Enlil uttered "breath of heaven," "breath of heaven,"

by their [word missing]. . . .it stretched itself,

Vegetation, coming up out of the earth, rises up.

Ziusudra, the king, prostrated himself before An and Enlil.

An and Enlil cherished Ziusudra,

Life like a god they give him:

Breath eternal like a god they bring down for him.

Then, Ziuusudra the king,

The preserver of the name of vegetation and of the seed of mankind,

In the land of crossing, the land of Dilmun, the place where the sun rises,

they caused to dwell.(4)

■ *YOUR INTERNET CONNECTION*

Are you aware that Egyptian hieroglyphics was also difficult for scholars to decipher? Like some cuneiform inscriptions in three languages found in Persia, by modern archaeologist, troops of Napoleon Bonaparte in 1799 found a basalt slab in hieroglyphic, demotic, and Greek. This great find called the Rosetta Stone, provided J.F. Champollion and others with the key to translating Egyptian hieroglyphic. Visit the web site of the great British Museum in London and see the stone and learn more about it.

`Http://www.british-museum.ac.uk/highligh.htm`

QUESTIONS

Now that you have read the document and followed the preceding steps, answer the three questions below:

1. Apply the categories used by the historian to organize information--what in the document is political history; economic history; social history; and so forth. For purposes of simplification, place abbreviations after appropriate sentences or statements in the two sections e.g. (p) political, (soc) social, (sci) scientific. Write directly in your workbook.

2. Upon completing the first question examine your results and re-read the document. Write a short paragraph describing what you think life was like in ancient Sumer. Use as many of the categories as you can to provide as complete a picture of this society as you are able. For example how important do you think the category of religion is based in the two sections? How would you describe this religion – monotheistic or polytheistic? As for social history what can you find about the place of men and women in the society under consideration? Do you think this civilization had an optimistic or pessimistic outlook on humans, on life? These questions are merely some examples of the ways you can use the categories and draw out information from documents. As you write your paragraph develop some of you're own questions using these as a guide.

3. Examine your results. Think about what you have done. Do you have a better understanding of history and what the historian does after completing this exercise?

Endnotes

1. Margaret Oliphant, <u>The Atlas of the Ancient World: Charting the Great Civilizations of the Past</u> (New York: Simon & Shuster, 1992), 67-69.

2. <u>Ibid.</u>, 76.

3. Samuel Noah Kramer, "The Sumerians," <u>Scientific American</u> (1957).

4. Samuel Noah Kramer, <u>History Begins at Sumer</u> (New York: Doubleday & Co., 1959), 108-109, 152-154.

Chapter III
A Basic Historical Skill - Selection

Theocracy, monarchy, tyranny, oligarchy, democracy--are you able to properly define these important terms? Do you know from what ancient civilization these terms are derived? If you answered the Greeks, you are correct! And of all of them, we most closely associate the Greeks with the last, democracy. In fact, it is often stated that the ancient Greek <u>polis</u> of Athens was the cradle of democracy; that many of the political ideals developed therein--equality among the citizenry, respect for the law, regard for justice, liberty--have been shaping forces in history up to the present.

Let us suppose you wish to examine the veracity of this claim regarding Athens and democracy. How would you go about doing it using the evidence provided in the following document? Remember to use your dictionary; to underline the key ideas; and, to put those ideas in your own words.

The word <u>democracy</u> entered English in the sixteenth century from the French <u>democratie</u>; the word is Greek in origin, having been derived from <u>demokratia</u>, the root meanings of which are <u>demos</u> (people) and <u>kratos</u> (rule). Democracy refers to a form of government in which, in contradistinction to monarchies and aristocracies, the people rule. It entails a state in which there is some form of political equality among the people . . . .(1)

In the course of examining the definition of democracy, the document, and the questions that follow them, you will engage in a most fundamental historical skill, the skill of selection. Consider what should take place. You will enter into a dialogue with the document--"a process by which the mind selects ever more accurately the sources that have significant meaning and relation to each other and at the same time refines the questions it needs to ask the sources."(2)

Think of it in another way by reflecting on the following problem relating to the Macedonian, Alexander the Great. Sometime in June, 323 B.C., Alexander, the man who extended Greek ideas and language to the ancient Near East, died. In that last year of his life, literally thousands upon thousands of things happened to him. Why have historians chosen to record so few of them?(3)

DOCUMENT

GENERATION OF ANIMALS

Aristotle

. . . The female, in fact, is female on account of inability of a sort, viz. it lacks the power to concoct semen. . . .

Now of course [in conceiving] the female, qua female is passive, and the male, qua male is active. . . .

. . . Wherever possible and so far as possible the male is separate from the female, since it is something *better* and more divine in that it is the principle of movement for generated things, while the female servers as their matter.

Young parents, and those which are older too, tend to produce female off-spring rather than parents which are in their prime; the reason being that in the young their heat is not yet perfected, in the older, it is failing.

Some offspring take after their parents. . . . Males take after their father more than their mother. . . . Others do not take after a human being at all in their appearance, but have gone so far that they resemble a monstrosity. . . .

The first beginning of this deviations is when a female is formed instead of a male, though (a) this indeed is a necessity required by Nature, since the race of creatures which are separated into male and female has got to be kept in being; and (b) since it is possible for the male sometimes not to gain the mastery either on account of youth or age or some such cause, female offspring must of necessity be produced by animals.

. . . While still within the mother the female takes longer to develop than the male does; though once birth has taken place everything reaches its perfection sooner in females than in males—e.g., puberty, maturity, old age—because females are weaker and colder in their nature; and we should look upon the female state as being as it were a deformity, though one which occurs in the ordinary course of nature.

- ### *YOUR INTERNET CONNECTION*

Read the original words of the founding Fathers at two wonderful institutions in Washington DC. Try both the Library of Congress and then the National Archives.
`http://www.library.byu.edu/~rdh/prmss/orte/washloco.html`
or their home page `http://lcweb.loc.gov/resdev/`
try `http://www/nara.gov/nara/naralibrary/govdocs/gdocs.html`

Were you surprised by the document by Aristotle? Want to learn more about women in the ancient world? If so, there is a web site for you. It is called Diotoma and it has information on the Study of Women and Gender in the Ancient World.
`http://www.uky.edu/ArtsSciences/Classics/gender.html`

QUESTIONS

1. Does Aristotle's discussion of women support or negate the idea that Athens was a democracy? Carefully, ever so carefully, select the appropriate evidence from the document.

2. Re-examine the definition of democracy as it was provided you at the beginning of this chapter. Given this definition is it possible that Athens was really a democracy? Explain your reasoning in a short paragraph.

3. How does the Athens of Aristotle compare with the democracy you are familiar with in the United States? Was it always the democracy with which you are currently living in today? Be prepared to discuss this in class.

- *CHALLENGE YOURSELF FURTHER*

    Examine the writing of some of the Founding Fathers of the United States. Did they believe in and practice democracy? Was it the same democracy you understand today? How was it different?

    Briefly trace the democratization of the United State political system.

Endnotes

1. Joel Krieger, ed., <u>The Oxford Companion to Politics of the World</u> (New York: Oxford University Press, 1993), 220.

2. Walter T. K. Nugent, <u>Creative History: An Introduction to Historical Study</u>, The Lippincott History Series (Philadelphia: J. B. Lippincott Company, 1967), 71, 72.

3. <u>Ibid.</u>, 72-74.

4. Aristotle, <u>Generation of Animals</u>, trans. A.L. Peck, The Loeb Classical Library (Cambridge, Mass.: Harvard University Press, 1943), p. 103; 113; 395-96;401-03; 406.

Chapter IV
Law Codes as a Historical Source

On desperate seas long wont to roam,
Thy hyacinth hair, thy classic face,
Thy Naiad airs have brought me home,
To the glory that was Greece
And the grandeur that was Rome.(1)

"The grandeur that was Rome." Surely you have heard that line from the poem To Helen by Edgar Allan Poe on numerous occasions and in a variety of contexts. Why? What exactly was the grandeur that was Rome? Have you ever thought about it? What would compel a poet, ever so many centuries later, to write such a line? Certainly it must have been something extremely significant. Recall the introduction to this great civilization in your text. If you are unable to do so, return to those pages and reread them. What did you find? Many things obviously, but one is there repeatedly--the ability to govern. This ability, many would agree, was greatly augmented through not only the establishment of political institutions but law. Consider the importance of these two factors working together simultaneously. Clearly this combination is of great importance because one alone, as in the case of the Greeks, was a source of weakness. This proved to be especially true when large political entities like empires were established. In short, it might be fair to say that the Greeks were great political theoreticians while the Romans were great political practitioners. As the Oxford University classicist William Ward Fowler (1847-1921) said of them, "The Romans were, in fact, the most practical people in history; and this enabled them to supply what was wanting to the civilization of the Mediterranean basin in the work of the Greeks."(2)

In light of the foregoing comments on Rome, it seems appropriate at this time to examine one of their law codes--the Twelve Tables. Before discussing their origins it should be stated that you will be asked to examine yet another code of laws later on. The reasoning behind this should be rather self-evident to you. Obviously law codes are an extremely important historical source. They can tell you a great deal about a civilization and its people. Looking at them from a comparative perspective also enables you to reflect on how societies differ; how they are similar; and perhaps, provide some insight into how they evolve over time. Keep this in mind as you read the Twelve Tables with your dictionary at your side.

As for the Tables, best evidence tells us they were compiled somewhere between 451-449 B.C. by a special commission of ten patrician magistrates. Originally inscribed on twelve bronze plaques (thus their name), the Tables were destroyed in 390 B.C. by the invading Gauls. Drawn up in response to pressure exerted by the other class in the early Roman Republic (remember who they were?), the Twelve Tables are of fundamental importance in reconstructing the history of this ancient time period.(3)

DOCUMENT

Selections from the Twelve Tables

Table III: Execution; Law of Debt

When a debt has been acknowledged, or judgment about the matter has been

pronounced in court, thirty days must be the legitimate time of grace. After that, the

debtor may be arrested by laying on of hands. Bring him into court.

If he does not satisfy the judgment, or no one in court offers himself as surety in his

behalf, the creditor may take the defaulter with him. He may bind him either in

stocks or fetters

Unless they make a settlement, debtors shall be held in bond for sixty days. During that time they shall be brought before the praetor's court in the meeting place on three successive market days, and the amount for which they are judged liable shall be announced; on the third market day they shall suffer capital punishment or be delivered up for sale abroad, across the Tiber.

Table IV: Rights of Head of Family

Quickly kill . . . a dreadfully deformed child.

If a father thrice surrender a son for sale, the son shall be free from the father.

A child born ten months after the father's death will not be admitted into a legal inheritance

Table V: Guardianship; Succession

Females shall remain in guardianship even when they have attained their majority.

If a man is raving mad, rightful authority over his person and chattels shall belong to his agnates or to his classmen.

A spendthrift is forbidden to exercise administration over his own goods . . . . A person who, being insane or a spendthrift, is prohibited from administering his own goods shall be under trusteeship of agnates.

Table VII: Rights Concerning Land

Branches of a tree may be lopped off all round to a height of more than 15 feet . . . . Should a tree on a neighbor's farm be bent crooked by a wind and lean over your farm, action may be taken for removal of that tree.

It is permitted to gather up fruit falling down on another man's farm.

Table VIII: Torts or Delicts

If any person has sung or composed against another person a song such as was causing slander or insult to another, he shall be clubbed to death.

If a person has maimed another's limb, let there be retaliation in kind unless he makes agreement for settlement with him.

Any person who destroys by burning any building or heap of corn deposited alongside a house shall be bound, scourged, and put to death by burning at the stake, provided that he has committed the said misdeed with malice aforethought; but if he shall have committed it by accident that is, by negligence, it is ordained that he repair the damage, or if he be too poor to be competent for such punishment, he shall receive a lighter chastisement.

Table IX: Public Law

The penalty shall be capital punishment for a judge or arbiter legally appointed who has been found guilty of receiving a bribe for giving a decision.

Table XI: Supplementary Laws

Intermarriage shall not take place between plebeians and patricians.(4)

QUESTIONS

After reading the introduction to this chapter and the document under investigation, you should be prepared to answer the questions that follow. Remember to write freely on the document pages as you use the procedures for analysis outlined in Chapter II.

1. Do you remember the categories the historian uses to organize information? -- political, economic, social, religious, scientific, and intellectual. Which of these do the Twelve Tables address? If you find more than one category identify them. If you find more than one example of a category select which you believe to be the best example.

2. Based on your study of the Roman Republic, are the Tables a good reflection of the society in question? How would you characterize that society using only the evidence in the document?

3. Based on the evidence provided in the document, would you describe the Twelve Tables as a comprehensive code of laws, that is, one embracing both private and public life? Explain your thoughts in a short paragraph.

4. After examining The Twelve Tables, do you have a better appreciation of your own legal system? Why?

Endnotes

1. <u>The Oxford Dictionary of Quotations</u>, 3rd ed., s.v. "Edgar Allan Poe 1809-1849."

2. W. W. Fowler, <u>Rome</u> (London: Williams and Norgate, 1912), 12, 55-59, 63.

3. M. Cary, <u>A History of Rome Down to the Reign of Constantine</u> (London: Macmillan & Co. LTD, 1965), 41-42.

4. Cicero, <u>Laws,</u> trans. C. W. Keys (Cambridge: Cambridge University Press, 1966) II, xii, 31.

Chapter V
Disagreeing With The Experts

At this point in your course of study, you should have examined two of the great religions of the world--Judaism and Christianity--along with a number of belief systems of other civilizations including Greek and Roman religion before the advent of Christianity and, prior to that, Zoroastrianism of the early Persians. Think back for a moment and try to recall anything about women in these religions. If you cannot, check the index of your text and reexamine the necessary pages with women in mind. Were women mentioned, and if so, in what context? How were they regarded? What role, if any, did women play in these religions--e.g., were they priestesses? Was there any sense of equality or inequality and on what premise was it based? These are important questions, if only in part because they continue to be issues debated within organized religion today.

Because it should be the most recently studied religion, the following exercise will focus on materials concerning Christianity and Paul of Tarsus (c.5 - c.67). Considered by many scholars to be the most important early Christian, Paul's attitudes regarding women and human sexuality continue to be debated. Dare to disagree with the experts as you examine the excerpts from the letters of St. Paul and two conflicting historical views. Have your dictionary by your side as you read the evidence and the questions that follow it. These questions should aid you in arriving at your own interpretation of Paul on women.

DOCUMENT 1

St. Paul

To the unmarried and to widows I would say this: it is an excellent thing if, like me, they remain as they are. Yet if they cannot contain, let them marry, for it is better to marry than to burn (with passion).(1)

Let those who have wives live as if they had none; let mourners live as though they were not mourning; let the joyful live as if they had no joy.

Man ought not cover his head, for he represents the likeness and supremacy of God; but woman represents the supremacy of man. Man was not made from woman, woman was made from man; and man was not created for woman, but woman for man. Therefore, in view of the angels, woman must wear a symbol of subjection on her head . . . . Is it proper for an unveiled woman to pray to God?(2)

Women must keep quiet at gatherings of the church. They are not allowed to speak, they must take a subordinate place, as the Law enjoins. If they want any information let them ask their husbands at home; it is disgraceful for a woman to speak in church.(3)

Wives, submit yourselves unto your own husbands, as unto the Lord.

For the husband is the head of the wife, even as Christ is the head of the church: and he is the saviour of the body.

Therefore as the church is subject unto Christ, so let the wives be to their own husbands in everything.

Husbands love your wives, even as Christ also loved the church, and gave himself for it;

That he might sanctify and cleanse it with the washing of water by the word,

That he might present it to himself a glorious church, not having spot, or wrinkle, or any such thing; but that it should be holy and without blemish.

So ought men to love their wives as their own bodies. He that loveth his wife loveth himself. For no man ever yet hated his own flesh; but nourisheth and cherisheth it, even as the Lord the church.

For we are members of his body, of his flesh, and of his bones.

For this cause shall a man leave his father and mother, and shall be joined unto his wife, and they two shall be one flesh.

This is a great mystery: but I speak concerning Christ and the church.

Nevertheless let every one of you in particular so love his wife even as himself; and the wife see that she reverence her husband.(4)

DOCUMENT 2

<u>Charles Seltman, Women in Antiquity</u>

Round about the middle of the 1st century of our era a new, idealistic, and utopian conception of the cosmos began to exert upon the civilized world a slow, leveling pressure . . . .

The observation has frequently been made that a [new] beginning . . . anti-feminism was due, in the first instance, to Paul of Tarsus . . . . Several factors require consideration: the background of Graeco-Roman civilization, with its real respect for women; the legal status achieved by women and their ability to fill responsible posts in civil life; the continuing love of female beauty expressed alike by poets, painters, and sculptors; and, lastly, a freedom in matters of sex . . . .

For a variety of reasons, all this really appears to have been repugnant to Paul of Tarsus. Conceivably the circumstances leading to his conversion had something to do with his attitude . . . . It has been suggested that the time which he spent in Ephesus between A.D. 52 and A.D. 54 had something to do with crystallizing his attitude toward women. In such circumstances, Paul, a genius in rebellion against society, was bound to run into trouble . . . . The letters to the Corinthians seem to reveal certain preoccupations that troubled Paul during his comparatively long residence in Ephesus. He had worries about money, idols, sex, and female liberty, and indeed he was most upset about sex and female liberty because he observed the absolute freedom, greater than anywhere else, enjoyed by the women of the city, and of all Ionia and Phrygia. But to Paul it all seemed great wickedness; and, endowed as he was with infinite courage, he dared to denounce it. His feeling came through in his letters from Ephesus to the churches of his foundation . . . .(5)

DOCUMENT 3

"Scholars Say Paul Wasn't Woman Hater"

That impassioned New Testament letter writer, Paul, often gets blamed by feminists these days for subordination of women. He's sometimes glibly denounced as a woman hater. But [some] scholars consider it a bum rap. They say that contrary to such popular images, Paul was a sensitive, affectionate man who recognized women's equal worth, whose views were ahead of his time, who worked closely with women and regularly extolled them.

"In his own time he was quite progressive about women," said the Rev. David Adams of Virginia Theological Seminary in Alexandria, Va., an Episcopal institution.

"He was very radical on their equality," Adams said. "To dismiss him as a misogynist . . . is just not so. He was not that at all."

Nevertheless, misinformed impressions of teachings considered by many scholars as mistakenly attributed to Paul sometimes get so warped that abusive husbands use them to justify beating their wives.

Claiming the Bible says wives are to be submissive, "they take the biblical text and distort it to support their right to batter," said U.S. Catholic bishops in condemning such domestic abuse of women. "A correct reading of Scripture leads people to a relationship based on mutuality and love."

The passage cited by the bishops as misused, Ephesians 5:21-33, apparently is not even Paul's. Scholars say that the books of Ephesians and Timothy, although purporting to be Paul's letters, have a distinctly different style and vocabulary than the huge corpus of authentic Pauline letters.

"Most scholars would say that the material is not from Paul himself," said Adams, a New Testament professor . . . .

But Adams said that while Paul expressed his basic radical stance on sexual equality, "there are other indications that at certain places he draws back . . . appropriating a kind of hierarchical view of society."

"It is fairly clear that he understood women were in a subordinate role, as did all of society," Adams said, adding this was "perfectly normal" in the historical context of Paul's culture.(6)

QUESTIONS

1. What is Paul's attitude about marriage and human sexual needs?

2. Can you determine the roles ascribed to men and women based on Paul's letters? On what foundation are these roles determined?

3. What did St. Paul describe as the proper relationship between husbands and wives? Are there conflicting points of view found in the selected excerpts? Is it possible to account for this variance of opinion?

4. What place did women have in the church, as outlined by Paul?

5. How do the historical interpretations of St. Paul differ?

6. Is it possible for you to determine how the historians in question arrived at their conclusions after reading Paul's actual letters yourself?

7. Now go ahead and do it--make your own interpretation of St. Paul on women. Do you think he was a product of his culture as the newspaper article states, or as Charles Seltman wrote in his book, Women in Antiquity, "a genius in rebellion against his society"?(7)

8. How is this exercise different from any other you have done so far? What kind of sources were used?

• *CHALLENGE YOURSELF FURTHER*

Chapter III in this workbook focused on a document by the great Greek philosopher Aristotle and his views on women. This chapter examined the early Christian leader St. Paul and his views on women. Go back to Chapter III and compare and contrast the views of these two important thinkers. How much do you think Aristotle may have influenced St. Paul? So you think Paul arrived at his own conclusions independently? If so, explain why, given what you have learned about early Christian thinking. Conclude by discussing how much, if at all, attitudes today reflect the views of these two important men.

Endnotes

1. I Corinthians 7:8-9.

2. I Corinthians 11:7-15.

3. I Corinthians 14:34-35.

4. Ephesians 5:22-33.

5. Charles Seltman, <u>Women in Antiquity</u> (London: Thames and Hudson, 1956), 184-188.

6. "Scholars Say Paul Wasn't Woman Hater," <u>The Plain Dealer</u>, 6 July 1993.

7. Seltman, <u>Women in Antiquity</u>, 184-188.

Chapter VI
What Do You Believe?

Throughout the foregoing chapters of this book, a very conscious attempt has been made to illustrate the point that history is an ongoing process involving intellectual skills of the highest order. In other words, that it is not the mere memorization of information, or what you may have learned to think of as the facts. Consider that if this were the case, historians could not disagree on St. Paul's attitudes about women and human sexuality as you learned they do in the previous chapter.

Historians disagree for very important and complex reasons, all of which cannot be addressed in these small volumes. This disagreeing, or "the lesson of historical criticism," is in fact a form of subtle doubting. Why is it important for historians to do this and for you, as a student of history, to understand the ideas behind it? Think about this as you read the thoughts of the British historian, George Kitson Clark, quoted below:

> No man can escape from history or for long ignore it . . . . Whether he likes it or not the results of history, or what purport to be the results of history, or opinions coloured by beliefs about history, will invade his life and mind. He must be prepared for opinions about history or historical experience to have deeply affected the mind of anyone with whom he has dealings. This being so it is the act of a wise man to come to terms with what he cannot evade, and bring it, if he can, under control; that is he must try to get as near as he can to the reality in the history with which he is confronted, to test the cogency of the historical opinions which are likely to influence his mind, or the minds of anyone who is important to him, and perhaps winnow some of the nonsense out of them . . . . to do this he must become a <u>critical historian</u> . . . .(1)

That in fact, becoming a critical historian, is your task in this chapter as you examine the life and works of the great Byzantine scholar Procopius. Procopius was Byzantium's 6th century historian and he wrote fourteen volumes recording the personages, politics, building projects, and military campaigns of the Emperor Justinian. Consciously modeled after the renowned Greek historian Thucydides' work on the Peloponnesian Wars, these works present a laudatory account of the Emperor's achievements. Sometime in the middle of completion, Procopius paused to author another work with an entirely different point of view about his employer, Justinian. The <u>Historia arcana</u>, or <u>Secret History</u>, was a scurrilous attack on the Emperor, his wife Theodora, the military commander Belisarius and his wife, Antonina. This history assembled "every scrap of gossip, surmise, scandal, and slander about the empress and court." Purposefully kept from publication, the work came to light early in the 17th century.(2) What could account for such variance in interpretation? Using the skills of subtle doubting, decide which of these views is the most accurate. Be able to explain why as you examine the evidence provided.

DOCUMENT

Thus it was that Theodora, though born and brought up as I have related, rose to royal dignity over all obstacles. For no thought of shame came to Justinian in marrying her, though he might have taken his pick of the noblest born, most highly educated, most modest, carefully nurtured, virtuous and beautiful virgins of all the ladies in the whole Roman Empire: a maiden, as they say, with upstanding breasts. Instead, he preferred to make his own what had been common to all men and, careless of all her revealed history, took in wedlock a woman who was not only guilty of every other contamination but boasted of her many abortions.

. . . .

And some of those who have been with Justinian at the palace late at night, men who were pure of spirit, have thought they saw a strange demoniac form taking his place. One man said that the Emperor suddenly rose from his throne and walked about, and indeed he was never wont to remain setting for long, and immediately Justinian's head vanished, while the rest of his body seemed to ebb and flow; whereat the beholder stood aghast and fearful, wondering if his eyes were deceiving him. But presently he perceived the vanished head filling out and joining the body again as strangely as it had left it.

. . . .

Later Mamilian also died. Anatolius's son-in-law, leaving one daughter who of course inherited his estate. While her mother was still living, this daughter too died, after marrying a man of distinction, by whom she had no children, male or female. Justinian immediately seized the whole estate, on the remarkable ground that it would be an unholy thing for the daughter of Anatolius, an old woman, to become rich on the property of both her father and her husband. But that the woman might not be reduced to beggary, he ordered her to be given one gold starter a day so long as she lived: writing in the decree by which he robbed her of these properties that he was granting her this starter for the sake of religion, "for it is my custom to do what is holy and pious."

. . . .

This, however, is worth telling among the innovations of Justinian and Theodora. Formerly, when the Senate approached the Emperor, it paid homage in the following manner . . . . It was not customary to pay homage to the Queen.

But those who were admitted to the presence of Justinian and Theodora, whether they were patricians or otherwise, fell on their faces on the floor, stretching their hands and feet out wide, kissed first one foot and then the other of the Augustus, and then retired. Nor did Theodora refuse this honor; and she even received the ambassadors of the Persians and other barbarians and gave them presents, as if she were in command of the Roman Empire: a thing that had never happened in all previous time.(3)

QUESTIONS

1. Go to your own textbook and at least three others. Read what each has to say about Justinian, Theodora, and Procopius. Note the significant events in their lives; their backgrounds; and, their achievements.

2. After reading the excerpts that precede these questions, find those things that cause you to either believe or doubt the accuracy of the <u>Secret History</u>. Don't forget to use your dictionary and to follow the steps for successful document reading.

3. Procopius, Justinian, Theodora, all lived a very long time ago. Are these issues regarding how you interpret their lives important today? How have those in the employment of contemporary American Presidents dealt with these issues? Why would it be difficult to be a "court historian" and still engage in subtle doubting?

4. An even more complex issue involved is the art of historical biography. In fact the matter is so thorny that another chapter will deal with it in depth. For now, think about the following quote and write a two hundred word essay agreeing or disagreeing with the thesis.

> . . . . The transgressive nature of biography is rarely acknowledged, but it is the only explanation for the biography's status as a popular genre. The reader's amazing tolerance . . . makes sense only when seen as a kind of collusion between him and the biographer in an exciting forbidden undertaking: tiptoeing down the corridor together, to stand in front of the bedroom door and try to peep through the keyhole.(4)

Endnotes

1. Geoge Kitson Clark, "The Critical Historian," <u>The Dimensions of History: Readings on the Nature of History and the Problems of Historical Interpretation</u>, ed. Thomas N. Guinsburg (Chicago: Rand McNally & Company), 17-18.

2. "Crowned Courtesan," <u>MD</u>, October 1966, 281.

3. Procopius, <u>Secret History of Procopius</u>, trans. Richard Atwater (Chicago: Pascal Covici Publisher, 1927), 111; 132; 266; and, 275.

4. Janet Malcolm, "The Silent Woman - I," <u>The New Yorker</u>, 23 & 30 August 1993, 86.

Chapter VII
Historical Generalization

In the two preceding chapters you have been grappling with issues centering on interpretation as a part of the historical process. Another extremely important component in this process is that of making generalizations. Can you define this term as it applies to history? Now read the following: "Theoretically, a historical generalization is a statement or term which has been inferred inductively from a number of particular cases, instances, or events."(1)

This definition of generalization should have taken you full circle intellectually-- right back to our beginning chapter where it was discovered that the definition of history meant a process of inquiry. To put this concisely, "the historical generalization suggests some regularity or pattern of events, ideas, and human actions which is of historical significance."(2)

Stop here and test your ability to recall and apply what you have learned from these exercises and the information in your text. What very famous ancient historian was attempting to use a historical generalization when he wrote "it will be enough for me . . . if these words of mine are judged useful by those who want to understand clearly the events which happened in the past and which (human nature being what it is) will at some time or other and in much the same ways, be repeated in the future. My work is not a piece of writing designed to meet the taste of an immediate public, but was done to last for ever."(3) Identify the generalization that has been made by rephrasing it in your own words.

Most historians agree that generalizations vary in gradations of inclusiveness. The simplest forms are one word labels--Jews, Christians, Muslims.(4) A more complex form of generalization serves to connect and interpret information. Obviously this level of use is extremely important for historical investigation. Not only does it put concepts and facts into meaningful relationship, it also helps to establish why and how certain events took place.(5)

Other forms of generalization operate at higher levels, but historians are not so prone to use them because they are quite unreliable. Our quote from Thucydides would be an example of a generalization of the highest degree of inclusiveness. Is he not seeking to find underlying principles of human behavior? Reread the quote.

Now examine the documents that follow. Each one is taken from three of the great religions in the world that you should have studied by this time in your course work. Follow the procedures you have used in the past as you work your way through the materials.

DOCUMENT 1

Psalm 8

O Lord, our Lord,

> how majestic is thy name in all the earth!

Thou whose glory above the heavens is

> chanted

> by the mouth of babes and infants,

> thou hast founded a bulwark because of thy

> foes,

> to still the enemy and the avenger.

When I look at thy heavens, the work of thy

fingers,

the moon and the stars which thou hast

established;

What is man that thou art mindful of him,

and the son of man that thou dost care for him?

Yet thou hast made him little less than God,

and dost crown him with glory and honor.

Thou hast given him dominion over the works

of thy hands;

thou hast put all things under his feet,

all sheep and oxen,

and also the beasts of the field,

the birds of the air, and the fish of the sea,

whatever passes along the paths of the sea.

O Lord, our Lord

how majestic is thy name in all the earth!(6)

DOCUMENT 2

The Gospel According to St. John

In the beginning was the Word, and the Word was with God, and the Word was God. The same was in the beginning with God. All things were made by him; and without him was not any thing made that was made. In him was life; and the light of men. And the light shineth in darkness; and the darkness comprehended it not.

There was a man sent from God, whose name was John. The same came from a witness, to bear witness of the Light that all men through him might believe. He was not that Light, but was sent to bear witness of the Light, that all men through him might believe. That was the true Light, which lighteth every man that cometh into the world. He was in the world, and the world was made by him, and world knew not him. He came unto his own, and his own received him not. But as many as received him, to them gave he power to become the sons of God, even to them that believe on his name: which were born, not of blood, nor of the will of the flesh, nor of the will of man, but of God. And the Word was made flesh, and dwelt among us (and we beheld his glory, the glory as of the only begotten of the Father), full of grace and truth.(7)

DOCUMENT 3

The Koran

Say: HE IS ONE GOD:

God the Eternal.

He begetteth not, nor is begotten;

Nor is there one like unto Him.

Magnify the name of thy LORD, THE MOST HIGH,

Who created, and fashioned,

And decreed, and guided

Who bringeth forth the pasturage,

Then turneth it dry and brown.

We will make thee cry aloud, and thou shall not forget,

Except what God pleaseth; verily He knoweth the plain and hidden.

And will speed thee to ease.

Admonish, therefore--verily admonishing profiteth,--

Who so feareth God will mind;

And there will turn away from it only the wretch

Who shall broil upon the mighty fire,

And then shall neither die therein, nor live.

Happy is he who purifieth himself,

And remembereth the name of his Lord, and prayeth.(8)

QUESTIONS

1. How many generalizations are you able to make about the documents?

2. Make different levels of generalizations from these documents. Is this more difficult to do? Think about the reasons and explain them in a paragraph or two.

3. With the three documents in mind, read the quote provided below and identify the type of generalization it makes.

    > Most men . . . do not think that men are all that matters.
    > To think this is to run counter to a very deep feeling,
    > namely, that man depends for life and fullness of being on
    > forces outside himself that share in some sense his own
    > nature and with which he must be in harmony. The
    > harmony thus sought is sometimes a harmony in action . .
    > . or it is a moral and spiritual harmony . . . or the harmony
    > sought is more than a harmony, it is a complete and final
    > identity . . . .(9)

4. Based on your reading of the documents, would you maintain that the above quote is an accurate generalization? Explain why or why not.

Endnotes

1. Lester D. Stephens, <u>Probing the Past: A Guide to the Study and Teaching of History</u> (Boston: Allyn and Bacon, Inc., 1974), 66.

2. <u>Ibid</u>.

3. Thucydides, <u>History of the Peloponnesian Wars</u>, trans. Rex Warner (Harmondsworth, England: Penguin Books, 1972), 324.

4. Walter T. K. Nugent, <u>Creative History: An Introduction to Historical Study</u>, The Lippincott History Series (Philadelphia: J. B. Lippincott Company, 1967), 76.

5. Stephens, <u>Probing the Past</u>, 68.

6. Revised Standard Version of the Bible (Division of Christian Education of the National Council of the Churches of Christ in the USA, 1971).

7. George H. Knoles and Rixford K. Snyder, eds., <u>Readings in Western Civilization</u>, 3rd ed. (Chicago: J. B. Lippincott Company, 1960), 170.

8. Stanley Lane-Poole, <u>The Speech-and-Table-Talk of the Prophet Mohammed</u> (London: Macmillan, 1905), 15; 32; 83; 133-137.

9. John B. Noss, <u>Man's Religions</u>, 3rd ed. (New York: The Macmillan Company, 1963), 3.

Chapter VIII
Comparing and Contrasting Historical Documents

In his famous work <u>Germania</u> written in A.D. 98, the Roman senator, consul, and author Tacitus stated:

> It is a duty among them to adopt the feuds as well as the friendships of a father or a kinsman. These feuds are not implacable; even homicide is expiated by the payment of a certain number of cattle and of sheep, and the satisfaction is accepted by the entire family, greatly to the advantage of the state, since feuds are dangerous in proportion to a people's freedom.(1)

Specifically Tacitus was referring to the vendetta or blood feud, long a practice among the various Germanic tribes of Europe. Originating with Iron Age peoples between 800-500 B.C. in the southern reaches of Scandinavia and northern sections of central Europe, the Germans lived in a society where custom determined all behaviors. This, plus the fact that they could not write until converted to Christianity sometime late in the 6th century, leaves historians with little factual information except for authors such as Tacitus. His work, quoted above, is frequently referred to as a "conscious idealization of a primitive and unspoiled people calculated to chasten and reform the decadent Romans."(2)

However true this characterization, much of what this first century Roman historian wrote has proven invaluable to understanding the German way of life and the legal system that resulted from it. Having no concept of statehood as you understand it to exist in the world today, the Germans lived in a basic social unit called a tribe. The <u>folk</u>, members of the tribe, were all united by blood lineage that descended from a common ancestor. Kin protected kin and legal customs were passed down from generation to generation through oral tradition. Each tribe had its very own customs and all members were subject to its rule no matter where they traveled. Various tribes, especially when on friendly terms, respected one another's laws.

Ruled by tribal kings or chieftains, these selected male members represented the strongest from among the folk. The test of strength was determined in battle. Emerging in combat, he in turn led in combat, settled disputes among his members, offered sacrifices to the various gods, and negotiated with those outside his own unit.

Influenced by Christian missionaries and by the Romans with whom they mingled, German customs and life gradually changed. Much of this change is reflected in the various codes of law, which the tribal leaders collected and recorded. These codes are not a coherent body of work, but rather an amended quilt--a works-in-progress, so to speak. Thus, they differ markedly from the previous law code you have examined in this volume. Remember what it was? Right, the Twelve Tables of the Roman Republic. You are reminded of these because in order to answer the questions in this chapter, it will be necessary to refer back to this earlier document.

The important historical skill of comparing and contrasting information is the focus of the exercise in this chapter. As a student of history you are often asked to do this in an examination question. Your professor is trying to teach you how to use information in a comparative way. Examine the following questions. Every one deals with the same historical problem, but each is treated in a different way because of the verb:

QUESTIONS

1. <u>Discuss</u> the role of law in Western civilization. Use the Roman Twelve Tables, and the Carolingian Capitulary Laws concerning Estates as the basis of your answer.

2. <u>Trace</u> the development of law in Western civilization using the Roman Twelve Tables, and the Carolingian Capitulary Laws concerning Estates as your chief pieces of historical evidence.

3. <u>Evaluate</u> the role of law in Western civilization using the Roman Twelve Tables, and the Carolingian Capitulary Laws concerning Estates as your examples.

4. Write an essay on the <u>effectiveness</u> of law in Western civilization. Make use of the following two law codes as your examples: The Roman Twelve Tables; and, the Carolingian Capitulary Laws concerning Estates.

5. <u>Compare and contrast</u> the role of law in Western civilization by using the Roman Twelve Tables, and the Carolingian Capitulary Laws concerning Estates.

Do you understand the importance of the point?

Interpret the documents that follow exactly as you have done in the past. Answer the questions that will be found after the documents.

DOCUMENT 1

<u>Alfred the Great Blood Feuds</u>

Also we enjoin, that a man who knows his adversary to be residing at home, shall not have recourse to violence before demanding justice of him.

1. If he has power enough to surround his adversary and besiege him in his house, he shall keep him therein seven days, but he shall not fight against him if he (his adversary) will consent to remain inside (his residence). And if, after seven days, he will submit and hand over his weapons, he shall keep him unscathed for thirty days, and send formal notice of his position to his kinsmen and friends.

2. If, however, he flees to a church, the privileges of the church shall be respected, as we have declared above.

3. If, however, he has not power enough to besiege him in his house, he shall ride to the ealdorman and ask him for help. If he will not help him, he shall ride to the king before having recourse to violence.

4. And further, if anyone chances on his enemy, not having known him to be at home, and if he will give up his weapons, he shall be detained for thirty days, and his friends shall be informed (of his position). If he is not willing to give up his weapons, then violence may be used against him. If he is willing to surrender and hand over his weapons, and anyone after that uses violence against him (the pursued), he shall pay any sum which he incurs, whether wergeld or compensation for wounds, as well as a fine, and his kinsmen shall forfeit his claim to protection as a result of his action.

5. We further declare that a man may fight on behalf of his lord; if his lord is attacked, without becoming liable to vendetta. Under similar conditions a lord may fight on behalf of his man.

6. In the same way a man may fight on behalf of one who is related to him by blood, if he is attacked unjustly, except it be against his lord. This we do not permit.

7. A man may fight, without becoming liable to vendetta, if he finds another (man) with his wedded wife, within closed doors or under the same blanket; or (if he finds another man) with his legitimate daughter (or sister); or with his mother, if she has been given in lawful wedlock to his father.(3)

DOCUMENT 2

Salic Law

If any person strike another on the head so that the brain appears, and the three bones which lie above the brain shall project, he shall be sentenced to 1200 denars, which make 300 shillings . . .

If any one have killed a free woman after she has begun bearing children, he shall be sentenced to 2400 denars, which make 600 shillings . . . .

If any one shall have drawn a harrow through another's harvest after it has sprouted, or shall have gone through it with a wagon where there was no road, he shall be sentenced to 120 denars, which make 30 shillings . . . .

But if any one have slain a man who is in the service of the king, he shall be sentenced to 2400 denars, which make 600 shillings.(4)

QUESTIONS

1.   What can you determine about Germanic society by examining their laws; of society in the Roman Republic under the Twelve Tables?

2.   How are the Germanic laws different from the earlier code of law? Account for these differences.

3.   How are the German laws similar to the early code of law? Explain the similarities.

4.   What concepts of abstract justice are included in these two law codes? Is it possible some are not based on such concepts? Can you explain why, based on the society(ies) in question?

- ***CHALLENGE YOURSELF FURTHER***

  Go further than the two examples of Germanic laws given and see what you can discover about the evolution of their various tribal laws. Do you find similar things in all of them as you compare and contrast them to the Roman Twelve Tables? Consult "The Burgundian Code," trans. Katherine Fisher Drew (Philadelphia: University of Pennsylvania Press, 1949); David Herlihy, ed., Medieval Culture and Society (New York: Harper & Row, 1968). How do you account for any differences among the various Germanic tribes?

Endnotes

1. Tacitus, <u>The Complete Works of Tacitus: The Annals o The History o The Life of Cnaeus Julius Agricola o Germany and Its Tribes o A Dialogue in Oratory</u>, ed. Moses Hadas, trans., Alfred John Church and William Jackson Brodribb, Modern Library Books (New York: Random House, Inc., 1942), 719.

2. Moses Brodribb, ed., <u>The Complete Works of Tacitus</u>, xii.

3. F. L. Attenborough, ed. and trans., <u>The Laws of the Earliest English Kings</u> (Cambridge: Cambridge University Press, 1922), 83-85.

4. E. F. Henderson, ed., <u>Select Historical Documents of the Middle Ages</u> (London: G. Gell & Sons, 1912), 176-189.

DOCUMENTS

Chapter II

From <u>History Begins at Sumner,</u> by Samuel Noah Kramer. Copyright © 1959 by Doubleday & Co. Reprinted with permission by Doubleday & Co.

Chapter III

From <u>Generation of Animals,</u> by Aristotle, trans. A. L. Peck. The Loeb Classical Library. Copyright © 1943 by Harvard University Press. Reprinted by permission of Harvard University Press.

Chapter IV

<u>The Twelve Tables</u>
From <u>Laws</u> by Cicero, trans. by C. W. Keys. Copyright (c) 1966 by Cambridge University Press. Reprinted by permission of Cambridge University Press.

Chapter V

Reprinted from the Holy Bible. New International Version. From <u>Women in Antiquity</u> by Charles Seltman. Copyright (c) 1956 by Thames and Hudson LTD. Reprinted by permission of Thames and Hudson LTD. "Scholars Say Paul Wasn't A Woman Hater," <u>The Plain Dealer</u>, 6 July 1993. Reprinted from <u>The Plain Dealer</u>.

Chapter VI

From <u>Secret History of Procopius</u> by Procopius, trans. by Richard Atwater, Copyright (c) 1927. Pascal Covici Publisher.

Chapter VII

From the Holy Bible. Revised Standard Version of the Bible. "The Gospel According to St. John," page 170. From <u>Readings in Western Civilization</u> by George H. Noles and Rixford K. Snyder. Copyright (c) 1960 by Harper & Row, Inc. Copyright renewed. Reprinted by permission of Harper/Collins Publishers, Inc. Reproduced with the permission of Macmillan Publishing Company, Inc. From <u>The Speech-and-Table-Talk of the Prophet Mohammed</u> by Stanley Lane-Poole. Copyright (c) 1905 by Macmillan Publishing Company.

Chapter VIII

<u>Alfred the Great Blood Feuds</u>
From <u>The Laws of the Earliest English Kings</u>. F. L. Attenborough, ed. and trans. Copyright (c) 1922 by Cambridge University Press. Reprinted by permission of Cambridge University Press.
<u>Salic Law</u>
From <u>Select Historical Documents of the Middle Ages</u>. E. F. Henderson, ed. Copyright (c) 1912 by G. Gell & Sons. Reprinted by permission of Harper/Collins Publishers, Inc.

Chapter IX

From <u>Beowulf,</u> ed. and trans. by Burton Raffel. Copyright (c) 1963 by The New American Library. Reprinted with permission of The New American Library.

Chapter X

From <u>Petrarca's Secret, or the Soul's Conflict with Passion</u> by Francesco Petrarca, trans. by William H. Draper. Chatto & Windus LTD. Random House UK LTD. From <u>Oration on the Dignity of Man</u> by G. Pico Della Mirandola, trans. by A. R. Caponigri. Copyright(c) 1956. Gateway.

Chapter XI

From <u>The Discovery of America, 1492-1584</u>, ed. by Philip F. Alexander. Copyright (c) 1917 by Cambridge University Press. Reprinted by permission of Cambridge University Press. From Amerigo Vespucci, <u>Mundus Novus</u>, trans. George Tyler Northrup, "Vespucci Reprints, Texts, and Studies," Vol. V. Copyright (c) 1916 by Princeton University Press. Reprinted by permission of Princeton University Press.

Chapter XII

Reprinted from <u>The Christian in Society</u> by Robert C. Schultz. Copyright (c) 1967 Fortress Press. Used by permission by Augsburg Fortress.

Chapter XIII

From <u>A King's Lessons in Statecraft: Louis XIV: Letters to His Heirs, Vol. II</u>, trans. by Herbert Wilson. Copyright (c) 1924 Ernest Benn Limited. Reprinted by permission of A & C Black Publishers Limited.